His Kentucky Smile
And an Ireland Dream

His Kentucky Smile
And an Ireland Dream

By Kip London

Edited by Penelope Fleming

Old Mountain Press

Published by:
Old Mountain Press, Inc
2542 S. Edgewater Dr
Fayetteville, NC 28303

www.oldmp com

© 1999 Kip London
Edited by Penelope Fleming
ISBN: 1-884778-71-2
Library of Congress Catalog Card Number: 99-63660

His Kentucky Smile And an Ireland Dream
Printed and bound in the United States of America All rights reserved. Except for brief excerpts used in reviews, no portion of this work may be reproduced or published without expressed written permission from the author or the author's agent.

First Edition
Manufactured in the United States of America
1 2 3 4 5 6 7 8 9 10

Acknowledgment

We, the loving family of Kip London, would like to extend our heartfelt appreciation to some of the people who have helped us, and who were a special part of Kip's life:

Penelope Fleming—a close friend of Kip's, Penny took responsibility for this publication project, editing and submitting his work; she also achieved a special memorial for Kip in Ireland.

Tiffany Parnell—drew the rune and preserved all of Kip's poetry on computer files

Metcalfe County High, class of '85—purchased the book <u>Ireland From the Air</u> in memory of Kip

We would also like to thank all the people who had trees planted in Kip's memory, as well as all his friends, co-workers, & volunteers at Horse Cave Theatre, KY; The Book Store in Horse Cave; friends at IU Southeast; the caring & compassionate Drs. Salisbury & Middleton; Winn Funeral Home; Charlie Williams & his staff; Quarry Hill Monuments; and especially Kip's close friends in various states across the country—you know who you are, and we want you to know that you will forever be in our hearts.

Those of his family who are in his heavenly company—Wayne, Tim, & Anthony—and those who survive him on earth—Rebecca, David, Micah, Cheryl, & Gidget(his poodle)—dedicate this book to the memory of Kip Jason London, that he may continue to touch the lives of others.

I know now what my purpose in this life is to be. I am to encourage . . . everyone is desirable, but there are those few who are special, and it is my task to make sure they know they are special and that they are capable of great things. I will always know when I must speak. I seem to have power within me, in that people do not like it when I am unhappy.

People also grow attached to me. This is a great honor, but also a burden. I should strive for happiness, for when I truly find it, I can help lead others to their own happiness.

—excerpt from KJL's journal

About the Author

Kip Jason London was born on May 29, 1967. A loving child, he grew into a caring adult. He attended Indiana University Southeast and graduated with a degree in History & Communications. Kip also worked part-time as a disc jockey for an Indiana radio station.

Encouraged by his college friends, Kip tried acting and discovered not only did he love it, but he was a natural. His first role was as Dr. Einstein in a production of Arsenic and Old Lace at IU Southeast. He also appeared in Holy Ghosts, The Shawl, and K2 while still at school.

After college, Kip began his journey into the acting profession in earnest. He was cast by Indiana's Clarksville Little Theatre as Ellard Simms in their production of The Foreigner; he won an award for Best Supporting Actor for that role. He went on to join Kentucky's Horse Cave Theatre as a production assistant. Kip remained at Horse Cave Theatre for several seasons, performing in numerous plays, and in his sixth and final season, he became eligible for and joined the Actor's Equity Association. Earlier that same year Kip performed with For a Good Time Theatre in Michigan, a children's theatre company that toured with their plays to elementary schools throughout the state.

Kip brought many special skills to the stage; he juggled, knew stage combat, and spoke several dialects, including German and British. In his personal life, he exhibited various other talents, particularly a knack for drawing people to him with his sensitivity and kindness. Kip met many people through his travels, and he took delight in corresponding not only with them, but with pen pals he had not met.

A true Kentucky Wildcat fan, he also loved nature and the simple things in life, as is obvious from his poetry. His poems were his way of expressing his remarkable insights about human nature and the workings of the world, and most are based on his own personal feelings and experiences. Music, too, was a major force in his life, and Kip spent many hours learning to play the guitar. Irish music held the greatest appeal for him; in fact, Kip was enamored of Ireland and wanted to visit someday. He hoped to publish his poetry and write a novel there. Towards that end, he began to study Irish history and how to speak Gaelic.

Kip thought of his life as a journey. He was never without a necklace made for him by a friend; the rune inscribed on the stone pendant stood for "journey". Kip entered a different stage along his journey when on August 11, 1997 he died in an automobile accident. His last performances were at Horse Cave Theatre in <u>Run for Your Wife</u> and <u>It Runs in the Family</u>, and he had been scheduled to appear in <u>The Miracle Worker</u>. His death was devastating to all who knew him, and so it became important to preserve and share the poetry he left as his legacy, the gift of his words that you now hold in your hand.

Kip was and always will be remembered as a special son, brother, and friend . . . To live in the hearts we leave behind is not to die.

Contents

To a Stranger Passing Through the Hills 23

Bizarre Intrepid Inside Myself Blazing Unhappily 24

Ireland Dream 25

One Second From Eternity 26

This Poem Has No Meaning 27

We 28

If Only You Were Here 29

Coffee House Blues 30

Landscapes 31

Lessons in Futility 32

Circle Completed 33

In Your Absence 34

The Storm 35

Strawberry Yogurt and Vanilla Lace 36

No Door For Me 37

Far 38

Long Awaited 39

One 40

Cycle of Discontent	41
My Spirit	42
Victory	43
Dream Dance	44
Mythic Proportions	45
Since You've Been Gone	46
Tears Enough For All	47
The Beckoning	48
3 Ks to Mardi Gras	49
A Place I've Dreamed Of	50
Ghost Town	51
Lost	52
Starlight for Rebecca	53
Reality	54
Sand Story	55
I Wrote This for Christine	56
All That Sparkled in My Eye	57
Going Home	58
Druid Moon	60
The Funeral	61

Last Sigh 62

Good Indian 63

The Sun Is Friend 64

She 66

Gossamer Wings 67

Metamorphosis 68

Homecoming 69

State of Being 70

The River 71

Departure 72

For Leslie Ann, My Best Friend 73

Do You Remember When We Ate Chinese? 74

Daydream 75

Nikki's Gifts 76

My Question 77

Your Reply 77

Let the Promise Die 78

Heritage 79

From Chicago to Louisville 80

Barbara's Simple Little Poem 81

Being Someone 82

Remembering	84
Autumn	85
Baile en Luna (Moondance)	86
Reflections	87
Across a Thousand Lifetimes	88
Night in Arizona	89
When All Your Dreams Have Left You	90
Winter Ballet	91
Grate Dreams	92
Still Life	93
Another Cliched Nature Poem	94
The Picture in Time	95
Malicious Whispers	96
Neon Strangers	97
October	98
Rebirth	99
Everything	100
Alchemy in Flames (The Marriage Poem)	101
For Lynn	102
Thoughts of You	103

My Friend	104
Poet's Wine	105
Rain	106
Gemini	107
With Me	108
Flying Too Close to the Sun	109
Emotional Hypothermia	110
Christine's Moon	111
Annie's Lives, Part I: *Of Sunshine and Angels' Wings*	112
Annie's Lives, Part II: *Mother*	113
Annie's Lives, Part III: *Hell*	114
Annie's Lives, Part IV: *Asylum*	115
Annie's Lives, Part V: *The Past Is Just That*	116
Anastasia	117
An Evening Remembered	118
Ageless Valentines	119
You Bring the Sun	120
When Words Lie Sleeping	121

To Penny and Wes 122

Poet's Moon 123

Night Music 124

Just for Chris 125

Inside 126

In Between 127

If I Never See You Again 128

Good Morning 129

East Panda Philosophy 130

Of Kip and Kindness—A Lullaby for You 132

To a Stranger Passing Through the Hills

I cannot discuss the styles of Rembrandt or Picasso,
but I can show you a wild deer
chewing clover beneath a fiery Kentucky sunset.
I am poorly versed in New Age philosophy
for all my thoughts are tied to the ageless, coal-choked hills.
I cannot give you high society,
but there is art in the graceful contour of a horse's flank
as it stands framed against an August storm cloud.
And every day
leather-necked philosophers gather at the country store
and talk of subjects older than Aristotle
and younger than the hard-packed earth they sit on.
All this I offer,
take from it what you will.
Only give something in return.
Leave a little of yourself,
a New Age infusion
to link yesterday with tomorrow
so the country store philosophers can speak of today.

Bizarre Intrepid Inside Myself Blazing Unhappily

Bizarre intrepid
save my soul
as I would you
longing to tell how
life is black
and no one
sees the key
I can see inside myself
it's out I cannot fathom
they tell me out is light
but how am I to know
when all is black within
Blazing unhappily
on full moon
Thursdays
caught in the grip
of some black
Insanity
This is the
fastest motionlessness
I've ever known.

Ireland Dream

Fireflies in night, emerald on black,
tiny jigsaw pieces of Ireland in my dreams.

Hanging on the clouds like a half-closed eye,
the moon lies back—wide-gapped mouth
thunders and snores.

Through my own half-lidded gaze,
I'd swear the man is smiling through the outburst.
Maybe he too knows that clouds aren't forever,
but come and go like dreams of faraway lands.

One Second From Eternity

Countless nights
I have cried in silence,
while thoughts of you
glowed like moonbeams
against the darkness of my mind.
Empty days
when the light of the sun
never reached inside of me.
If I could wring one second from Eternity,
it would be the
timeless moment
when your sea blue eyes
flamed my soul
and
you breathed "I Love You"
into my heart.

This Poem Has No Meaning

This poem has no meaning.
There's nothing left to say,
So I'm saying that . . . exactly.
Search for meaning among the clouds
making faces in the sky.
Find your wisdom in the river
that moves constantly away from us,
to lose itself in something bigger.
Don't look for it here.
I stopped philosophizing
when my pretensions drowned
in the lullaby showers of April.

We

The conversation's easy
between myself and me.
Sometimes we argue,
but we never hold a grudge.
He doesn't mind too much
when I interrupt,
because he knows he'll get his turn.
Others don't understand.
It's ok they say,
to talk to yourself,
if you don't answer back.
But it's crazy
I say to me,
to talk when no one's there.
True, says me,
If you weren't here
I'd be insane.
Ah, he's a sharp one,
that fellow I call me!

If Only You Were Here

The silver moon looks good enough to eat,
but
you're not at my table.
The stars resemble perfect skipping stones
but
you're not on my river.
The sun would blaze in my fireplace
if only you were here to strike the match.
When you return
we'll gather armloads of night
and fistfuls of blue sky
and burn them like incense
on the altar of our smiles.

Coffee House Blues

Gray walls of smoke,
rattle of cup on saucer,
my nerves tremble like guitar strings.
I long for a quiet corner
away from the smoke that stains the air
and people's voices.
Away from pretentious wisdom
and maturity,
and all things New Age.
I crave silence
but it went out with Courtesy
and lies there still,
voiceless in its longing.
I want to go home and gorge myself
on solitude.
But wait . . . who's that with the steamy mocha eyes,
and such hair,
cascading in deep auburn ringlets
over her bare white shoulders?
That face,
demure sunlight under shadow.
Signal the waiter for another espresso.
Home lies there,
in that shy, raspberry-flavored smile.

Landscapes

Scattered moments
lie frozen in the icy landscape of my mind.
Some I walk past with barely a glance,
others I regard with detachment,
long past the pain of experience.
I slide to a stop as I come to the newest scenes,
not yet frozen,
but bleeding my psyche scarlet
with the last bitter drops.
There I am,
pinned to a wall with metal daggers
all of your design.
And there you are,
amazed at the jagged wounds,
not knowing it was you who threw the blades.
Someday you'll walk in your own secret place
and bandage the cuts I left in your soul,
some intended, still others never dreamed of.
And when these latest memories
have frozen over the pain,
perhaps we'll wander into the same spring garden
and start again,
like April's newborn daffodils.

Lessons in Futility

That solitary cloud in the sky is me
nudged wherever by whatever wind
just waiting to dissipate

I'm the hot metal in the forge
beaten and hammered
shaped by hands not my own

There I am in ripples on the pond
uneven waves reaching out to nothing
slowly moved to stillness

I was the memory that surfaced in your mind
forced down and supplanted
pushed back 'til it disappeared

Circle Completed

A soft-souled warrior,
he stands in the middle
of a life he built with his own callused hands.
His heartbeat,
the thud of hammers,
and his pulse,
the rasp—silence—rasp of a deep-cutting saw.
A far-seeing man,
his gift for reading
lies beyond mere symbols on a page.
A true life artisan,
he helps us carve the runes of our individual selves,
and gives us visions of who we are
and who we might become.
An ageless friend,
he walks beside us
and completes our spirit-forged circle.

In Your Absence

In your absence
my heart is folded like
a seagull's wing.
Tucked neatly
in the corner of my soul,
it waits
for your return.

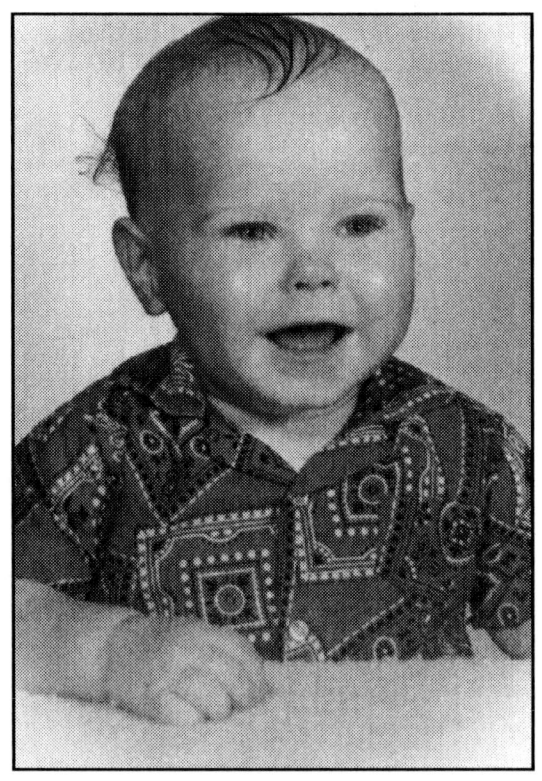

The Storm

I rose to greet the storm.
I could hear her mumbling in the distance.
She was black as pitch as she ran frantically toward me.
She was close now, and no longer mumbling, but shouting.
I felt her breath as she drew ever closer.

As she approached, the small cedars,
and tall weeds bowed to her.
As she came to me she began to cry.
Her cool tears fell on me slowly at first,
then pelted me as she grew sadder.
She stayed there for a while, letting everything
feel the violence boiling within her.
Her eyes flashed brightly,
bathing the fields in a blue-tinged glow.

Presently she stopped. Her angry shouting turned now
to a low muttering.
She was no longer flushed black and angry, but gray,
as if all her emotions had been spent.
Her eyes, which had once lit the world,
now merely sparkled in the distance.
She walked away slowly, as if reluctant to leave.

Strawberry Yogurt and Vanilla Lace

I wonder what you're doing at this moment.
Maybe you're eating strawberry yogurt on the bed.
or
emerging from the tub in a sheen
of vanilla lace.
Maybe you're thinking what a crud I am
for not understanding that
Coals burn slowly before
they glow red.

No Door For Me

How can I stand close to you
when your eyes are so far away?
And what do you see
when you daydream?
Perhaps a rich man in a house
with no door for me,
or maybe a white-tipped mountain
that I cannot climb.
I have thought to embrace you
but my arms won't hold
your discontent.
Will I lose you then
as the trees have lost their color?
I wish I could see what
holds your eye for so long a time;
if not to change it,
at least to understand.
Finally, your eyes return to the room.
You look at me
and snow begins to fall.

Far

The pink moon looks fragile,
that I might
shatter it with a stone.
But it is far,
unreachable as your heart.

Long Awaited

My happiness
cannot be measured like falling snowflakes.
Felt for,
it cannot be touched
like a raindrop
splashing softly in my palm.
Listening,
I cannot hear it
like the wind
sighing through the bare winter branches.
But so long awaited,
it is easily seen
when thoughts of you
burst into smiles.

One

Surroundings fade
as I'm drawn into your hazel eyes.
I stare through them
that I might find myself on the other side,
listening
to hear my name
in the music of your voice.
I want to step inside you,
To be wrapped in you.

Cycle of Discontent

Wish for winter snow in summer
Wish for warmth when cold comes
Always wanting what's never there
is no one content simply to be?

Wanting someone to share with
complaining when we have to give
Wanting it all
griping about too much to take care of.

Wanting more time
there's nothing to do when we get it
People compete to see who suffers most
only being happy when they're not happy.

My Spirit

Sometimes in daydreams I send my spirit
flying over green meadows.
Not caring to soar with eagles, I flit about
with swallows, who are much more fun.
Sometimes my spirit wanders into the cities,
running in and out of traffic, smiling at angry drivers—
not immune if a car should catch me unaware,
for where the fun without the danger?
Sometimes my spirit swims,
disdaining the oceans and larger swimmers
to play tag with quicksilver minnows
in the inexorable push of the river.
Fun is found in little things,
devoid of self-importance and higher meaning.

Victory

Ragged breath, my wounds are bleeding
my body ripped and torn
death is closing ever faster
to die and be reborn

The dragon circles once, then twice
his shrill cry cuts the air
no one else to slay the dragon
I alone take the dare

Talons flashing bright and fast
the dragon closes in
he screams his rage and scatters fire
the bane of mortal men

My sword comes up and slices clean
the blood of dragons flows
the monster takes a mortal hit
but hardly even slows

He backs away and tries again
his pent-up rage released
I steel my nerve to strike again
and try to stay the beast

My blade cuts into dragon flesh
the final die is cast
now coughing, thrashing on the ground
the dragon dies at last

My blood is flowing freely now
my body cold as stone
I don't resist impending death
the victory has been won

Dream Dance

The stars were twinkling stepping stones
against the dark sea of the sky.
We watched the moon
float over the horizon
like an orange balloon.
Below us,
the lights of the city
were a blanket of candles spread over the valley.
The green glow of lightning bugs
outlined the trees.
On a floor of fragrant pine needles
we danced to the music
in our hearts.

Mythic Proportions

I went looking for god,
but not one deity could I see—
until I looked inside my soul
and found god's eyes looking out through me.

I went looking for heaven,
wondering vainly where it could be—
imagine my complete surprise
when I found it here inside of me.

God and heaven are here and now;
We don't need Christian eyes to see—
Jesus said in metaphor
there is no god but you and me.

Since You've Been Gone

The stars don't shine like they used to
since you've been gone
the sun won't dry my tears
since you've been gone
The nights and days are unchanging
time never moves without you by my side
I'm only half who I used to be
my heart grew cold and the fire in me died.

Since you've been gone
my heart's flown away
oh will these lonely nights ever end
because I know that I can't live
until your hand is in my hand again.

The man in the moon ain't been smilin'
since you've been gone
the poetry has stopped rhymin'
since you've been gone
But one of these days you'll come back to me
and turn my gray sky back into blue
I'll take you gently by the hand
and show you how much I love you.

Since you've been gone
my heart's flown away
oh will these lonely nights ever end
because I know that I can't live
until your hand is in my hand again.

Tears Enough For All

Sweet Michelle,
you have tears enough for all.
It's OK to cry for the world
if you can also wear its smiles.
This place is so much nicer
when filled with your laughter.
If I could, I would draw the pain from you
and fling it from my fingertips;
failing that I will simply cry with you.
And when you smile my tears will stop,
And tomorrow the honey-kissed sun will rise.

The Beckoning

Cold shudders tickled my body
as my eyes stared transfixed on the page.
I looked up for a moment,
and saw a specter framed in the darkness.
Luminous green eyes and white fangs strained red.
Those eyes, they beckoned to me.
I rose from my chair,
unable to wrest my gaze from his.
My brain screamed alarms,
but my heart would have me calm, unafraid.
I could not resist his unearthly pull,
nor did I wish to.
He spoke to me,
though his dull red lips made no movement.
His soft, melodic voice filled me with peace.
"I am Louis."
It was as if my reading of him
had brought him to me.
Not aware of having moved,
I stood suddenly before him.
I became aware of my heartbeat then,
Pumping his crimson feast.
I sensed his heartbeat,
in synchronicity with my own.
I was ready . . .

I awoke to the soft glow of the desk lamp
in the middle of the room,
my hand outstretched,
as if reaching for something . . .

3 Ks to Mardi Gras

You were drinking beer
in the lobby of the Best Western
when I walked in.
Three hours after slamming
my truck into a divider
I was drinking Busch beer
in your hotel room,
while we mapped out
states on our palms.
Later, we slid across the icy parking lot
to the "Dead Beat Club"
and talked to truckers
stranded by the ice.
The next day you drove me home.
Kristen driving through the slush,
Kendra wearing the glasses
stolen from the Dead Beat Club,
and Kim and I
sharing candy hearts in the back seat.
Standing on the porch of my house
I watched you roll off to Mardi Gras,
wishing I was going with you . . .
Thanks for the fun!

A Place I've Dreamed Of

You came of age
in a place I've only dreamed of.
I missed you sighing
with the ghosts who wander Little Round Top,
and I wasn't there
when you shattered puddles
in the Gettysburg rain.
What a lovely picture you must have made
sitting beneath a dogwood tree,
flame-woven hair
framed by spring's white blooms,
writing of carousels and candlelight.
I've missed all this and more.
So tell me your stories,
and let me laugh and cry
and lose myself
in your chameleon green eyes.

Ghost Town

Twilight settles itself around the broken-down shacks
The last sliver of orange peeks over the horizon
A chill creeps in as darkness approaches
A lone brown prairie dog observes the emerging stars
The silver thumbnail of the moo hangs over the valley
The hidden whippoorwill sings his song,
as if to say, "I too am here"
One can almost hear the tiny piano in the saloon
Faint echoes of voices stir the imagination
A little girl behind me says "hello",
I turn but no one is there
Childish laughter fades into the summer nights' breeze
My heart jumps as yellow cats' eyes reflect the moonlight,
two shining orbs framed in black
As I turn to leave a small voice faintly cries,
"Daddy . . . come back"

Lost

Brief chuckling interludes
crammed between fits of weeping
Pathetic sadness exudes from me
in waking and in sleeping
Once in a while a smile creeps in
but finds itself soon leaving
lost in a battle it cannot win
between happiness and grieving

Starlight for Rebecca

Orion still hunted the sky
as smiling,
I passed the house where Rebecca slept.
Perhaps she dreamed of Boston
as I passed beneath her window.
The stars were so low
I thought to touch them.
Maybe I could gather some
and make for her a gleaming necklace.
Radiant,
like her smile,
which gladdens me.

Reality

There is no reality, only shared perception
seeing only what we want to see
forsaking truth for familiarity

Images are everything, hiding reality
showing no one who we really are
building walls, remaining within

We feel a need to open ourselves
to show the true person we are
but the need to hide is greater

To tear down the wall, to expose our emotions
to reveal that which is hidden
the destiny to which we must aspire

Sand Story

Bones lie in the sand
bleached white by the sun
Broken, they thrust upward like knives

Heat waves shimmer, marking the distance
A cactus ahead flickers large, then small
its green body undulating in the sun

Trickles of sweat trace the contours of my face
my light-blue shirt is now soaked dark-blue
It clings to me as if it had fingers

The off-white sand pulls at my feet
like red coals clinging to bare skin
Floating black shadows fall all around me

I shiver as a breeze cools the sweat against my skin
A glance up shows black clouds gathering
Raindrops start to fall, I see no place to hide

I Wrote This for Christine

Two snowflakes
samely dissimilar, falling
side-by-side until we land
in different worlds.
I come to rest, a snowflake
with a distinctly different pattern.
You have left some of yourself in me,
to anchor me against chance winds;
to make my own breeze
and ride it where I will.
May your breeze be warm and gentle
and carry you back to me,
so that I might thank you
for the passion I will have become.

All That Sparkled in My Eye

You came to me with the heat of summer
with red-brown hair shining bright in the sun
gave me a new way to look at the world
put me together when I came undone.
The summer melted slowly into fall
the leaves turned bright as my love for you grew
everything faded away from my sight
'til all that sparkled in my eye was you.
The trees fell bare as winter drifted in
the days turned cold but love remained aglow
the nights were ours to hold each other through
and joy like wine from golden cups did flow
and as you leave from home amid my tears
remember that a part of me goes too
I cannot lose what I so freely give
so take my heart and carry it with you.

Going Home

Stone gray replaces pitch black
once fast and graceful
now slow and cautious

I used to run and jump
of frosty Autumn mornings
now a walker is my constant companion

I am now in the Winter of my life
I look back at Spring, Summer, then Fall
and I wonder, does my life have meaning?

Have I used it well, or only wasted it?
I will be gone before the question is answered
this mortal life will not reveal its secrets

I remember my wife
her hair of purest gold
hand-in-hand we trod the path of life

I am not saddened as I think of her
all the good times stream through my consciousness
she was the light that led me to my destiny

I think of my friends
all are gone now
I am alone but never lonely

In my heart they're always with me
standing at the end of a long tunnel

I move to greet them
my body regains its youthful form
I revel in my newfound strength

They surround me
all is bliss
as they welcome me home
Could It Be I'm Dead?

Weaving, bobbing, spinning
thoughts go through my head
circle, circle, mass confusion
could it be I'm dead?

My thoughts all scatter, leaves in wind
my vision turning red
spirits mutter profound wisdom
could it be I'm dead?

Hearing everything, hearing nothing
what was it that they said?
Someone tell me, oh please tell me
could it be I'm dead?

Spirit floats, no longer mine
my earthly body shed
I'm disjointed, freely flying
could it be I'm dead?

Druid Moon

The moon drips silver on the trees
as white-robed dancers form a circle.
The first tingle of magic flows in on
the evening's cool breath
and the dancers' eyes reflect the stars' pale fire.

The Funeral

Men in dark suits laugh raucously in a corner
women talk of who is cheating on whom
and children are themselves
soft music performs its subconscious task
a small group sits quietly alone
their senses dulled to stillness
a woman of black hair speckled with gray
bows her head and wonders
how this can be her son's funeral

Last Sigh

Desperate death
bleeds the soul
Thin red line
on creamy white wrist
Your life stains the floor
Memories gush with each heartbeat
Your eyes become panes of blue glass
with the last sigh of your lungs

Good Indian

Jimmy Littlefeather had a vision
His first waking memory
was his mother falling
a round hole above her right eye
He ran
screaming in the moonlight
Bluecoats on demon horses
slaughtered his people
One step away
from his secret hiding place
something slugged him in the back
His lifeblood
trickling from his mouth
Little Badger fell to his knees
One final tortured breath
and he became
a "good Indian"
Jimmy Littlefeather had a vision

The Sun Is Friend

Have you seen the sun, Florida girl?
It's playing hide-and-seek in the clouds.
It peeked at us briefly in Ann Arbor
as we laughed our way through crowded college stores.
Now it's hidden behind gray Michigan snow clouds.
I hope it smiles at us again,
for the sun is friend to misplaced southerners.
For now, our smiles at a day well-spent
will have to do,
as we remember Brecht monologues
and a little box of chocolates in a Greek restaurant.
And someday soon
we'll see the sun of home and family,
and the cruel Michigan winter
will run from the warm embrace of spring.

She

Ash-blonde hair with a tinge of red
with saucy, witty style
the beauty of her face is wed
to the brightness of her smile

Her laugh is one that charms my heart
like music to my ear
but I play the shy and clumsy part
whenever she is near

I often find I cannot speak
only mumble in despair
my head grows heavy, my knees get weak
life just isn't fair!

One day she will realize
what a joy that I could be
and I won't have to fantasize
she'll be right here with me

Gossamer Wings

You came to me with gossamer wings
and flew too soon away.
I was saddened by your leaving,
but stronger for having known you.
JOY,
LOVE,
PRIDE,
these things and more you were to me.
In your innocence
teaching me
things I never knew before.
Where you are,
do you think of me?
Because I never cease
to think of you,
my child

Metamorphosis

How proudly you once stood
white walls trimmed in red
columns supporting you like Atlas' arms

A long lane led up to you
lined by tall swaying oaks
hard-packed by many carriage wheels

Once you hosted cotillions
the men talked of horses and the hunt
the women shared secrets and idle gossip

The young belles' skirts rustled as they danced
swaying and gliding in their partners' arms
young couples moving in step with the music

Now no one lives within your blackened walls
no dancing or talking in the parlor
no music to be heard

You are one empty shell
the half-burned pillars still stand
but there is nothing left to support

Homecoming

Fog lays across the river like a white shroud
this place then must be a tomb
all the people incarcerated here are specters
ghosts from some forgotten age

I wander aimlessly among these lifeless shades
their blue and brown eyes unseeing, emotionless
a gray-haired woman screams that the world is ending
her feverish gaze chills me into numbness

I once walked among the living with a purpose
but now I find myself joining the spectral dead
my blue eyes stare listlessly, unknowing
I am swallowed into the ragged arms of my new family

State of Being

Crystalline thoughts shrouded in crimson haze
Purple illusions clash with green realities
Blue and gold ideas evolve
As gray and black doubts take their leave

The River

The river rolls past the sycamores
a pale-green carpet
scarlet leaves ride the current like tiny boats
one comes to rest against the muddy bank

From the bluff I can see
rainbow trout shimmering through the water
turtles float up from the bottom
their heads make ripples on the surface

on the bluff across the river
a fox lopes onto the edge
reddish fur turns crimson in the sun
he sniffs the air, then turns away

Shadows lengthen across the river
crickets start their nightly concert
one last look at the orange, red, and pink of sunset
the sounds of the river fade as I walk away

Departure

Her black hair bobbed up and down,
as she walked in slow motion out of my life.
I stretched and strained to keep her in sight,
But finally she was gone.

My heart felt as cold as the Alaska snow she headed for;
emptiness churned deep inside me.
I felt like my soul had just walked away with her,
leaving me a husk with only hurt inside.

A smile lights my face when I think of her,
but it tastes salty from the tear that follows.
Replayed over and over in my head,
her black hair blowing as she walks away.

For Leslie Ann, My Best Friend

I see her face mirrored in the purple egg she
gave me
Her black hair and light purple lipstick in
perfect contrast
Given and taken in friendship
As I grasp it in my hand,
I imagine that it is her hand in mine.

Do You Remember When We Ate Chinese?

Do you remember when we ate Chinese?
the waitress laughed when I said "hold the rice"
you lauded me for originality

The dark-green pea pods sat on a plate, untouched
we talked of babies and insecurities
you asked if you had chicken stuck in your teeth

The gray smoke from your cigarette curled around your head
your red hair glinted in the sun that came through the window
a perfectly framed picture of your smiling face

Daydream

Her hair is the color of straw from the field.
Her face is so soft and sweet.
Her skirt rustles when she walks
as if it had a voice of its own.
What is it about her that intrigues me?
She is cute, but that is a small part of it.
It is more the complete picture.
The way she carries herself shyly,
the way she looks about, as if she is unsure.
Something draws me to her,
something undefined that pulls me in her direction.
In my daydream I walk up to her and
take her hand in mine.
She looks into my eyes and all that I am
and have ever been is revealed to her;
two spirits intertwined.

Nikki's Gifts

When you laugh Nikki, the world laughs too,
for such sweet innocence is most compelling.
Let not the doubters silence your golden voice
for it can shatter the frowns of lonely souls,
and warm the nights of the cold of heart.
Give your gifts freely to all who would receive,
and love will ever whisper softly in your ear,
and the beauty of the world
will glow in your beautiful brown eyes.

My Question

If I gave you my heart would you hold it?
Shelter and comfort it?
or would you throw it coldly into the past
like all the other hearts
you have collected through years of emotional conquests?
Consider it carefully,
for I have only one heart to give
and would not surrender it lightly.

Your Reply

Give me your heart
that I might make of it what I will.
True love has naught to prove
and insecurity is ever static.
Each heart given to me
was sheltered and comforted,
and each walked blindly into the past
looking for the future.
Give me your heart
and out of yesterday and tomorrow
we'll fashion today.

Let the Promise Die

Fading into silence
let it drift away
funny how the colored moments
all have turned to gray
Let the promise die between you
the lover is all in your head
The passion you once lived for
is slowly falling dead
Let it fall from your eyes
watch it hit the ground
As it flows away forever
leaving darkness all around
The world moves on without you
the sun has left the sky
Rainbows made from falling teardrops
live long enough to die.

Heritage

Two blackened walls stand in mute defiance
their surfaces marred by bullet holes
reminders of a heritage lost

The once swaying live oaks are now skeletons
their bony arms sagging toward the ground
the long lane overgrown with a tangle of weeds

No one comes to visit anymore
a tribute to Sherman's nasty horde
you sit in silence through the ages

From Chicago to Louisville

I looked out over the wing
as the jet banked to the left.
I stared down
into a puffy frozen sea,
and splashes of blue water sky
shone through the clouds.
The jagged ridges of the clouds
looked like cotton candy mountains.
We descended into them
like a submarine into the ocean,
floating like a leaf
in a cool spring breeze.
Touching down was
like waking from a dream,
somehow no longer real,
but always remembered.

Barbara's Simple Little Poem

Dance,

        For life is short

                and you are strength.

Sing,

        For winter is here

                and you are warmth.

Laugh,

        For time is endless

                and you are love.

Being Someone

I look upon the rough brown boards of the stage
the set has been struck and it is bare
I long to be up there once again
being someone other than myself

The audience gives me a calmness
an assurance that I belong there
their response becomes my lifeblood
the sustenance on which I feed

The feeling onstage cannot be captured elsewhere
only there, within those small confines
can I be at one with myself
only there can I show the real me

Acting is a true paradox
a puzzle not meant to be solved
only when being someone else
can I truly be me

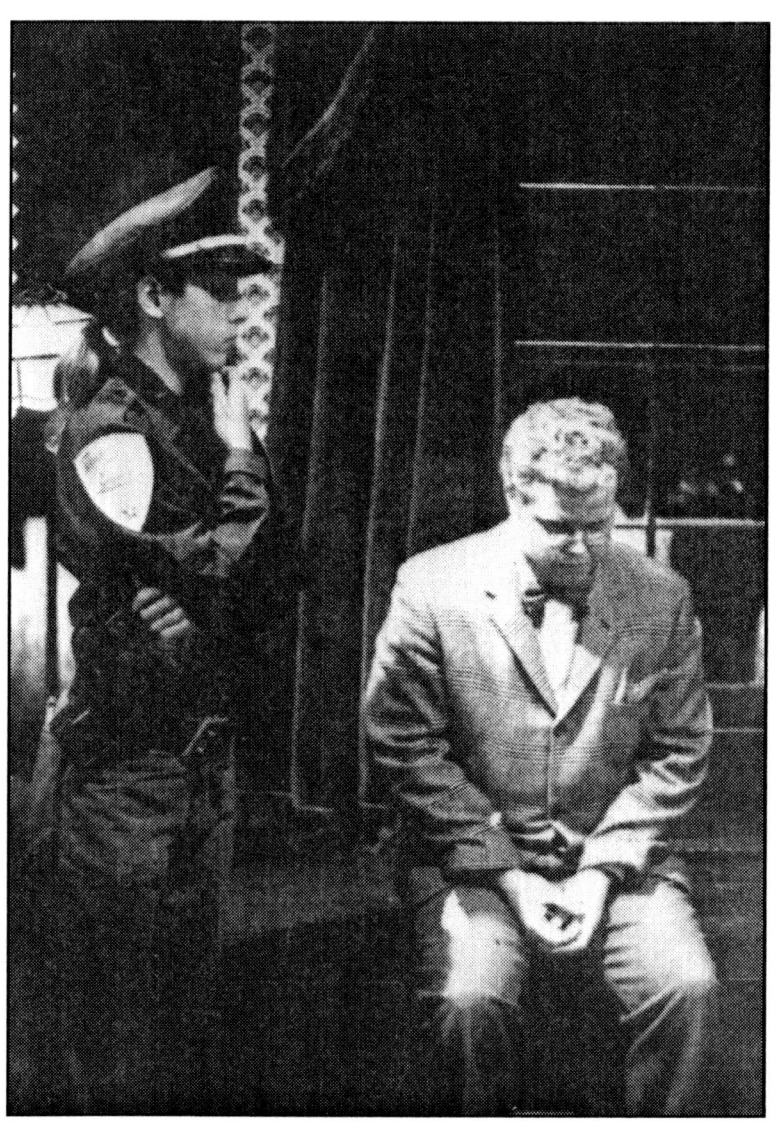

Remembering

Remembering times that I've sung and danced,
Laughed and cried, and begged for my sanity,
Times I was still. I love them all in my own way.
To forget the people and things that have made
Who I am, What I am, and Want to be
Would be a death of a most painful kind.
In the memories I love and hate,
All is contained.
When and if gone, you will never be far;
Forever you will live on within me.

Autumn

The breeze brings goosebumps to my arms
The leaves of autumn sway gently to and fro
Angry scarlet, gentle green, vibrant purple, soothing yellow
Some take flight, gliding gently to the ground
Others stay behind, not yet ready to face the unknown

The surface of the lake reflects the sunlight
A million shards of glass
Leaving green and blue imprints to closed eyes
Pale-green lily pads float on top of the lake
Like stepping stones to another world

The weeds in the field are brown and yellow
Waiting for white death to claim them
The grass is slowly turning brown
As it surrenders to the change of seasons

Baile en Luna (Moondance)

If I could,
I would shake the night sky
until the stars fall from it like rain.
I would pluck those shimmering lights
from the earth and
bring them to you.
Together we would stack them,
each atop the other,
until we stood upon the moon
and danced in its silver-blue glow.

Reflections

I remember walking down the street with you
I saw my reflection in your black sunglasses
the sunlight glinted off your purple warm-up suit

The smell of bread baking tickled our noses
a man in orange-colored robes walked past us
red, green, and blue banners filled the store windows

I spotted Abe Lincoln in the clouds and you laughed
we stopped at a restaurant and ate pizza
a circle with red polka dots surrounded by yellow

We walked again, down a cobblestone street
a little girl in a pink dress asked you for a quarter
the girl skipped off down the street; we were alone again

Across a Thousand Lifetimes
(based on Bach's ideas & themes)

If I cried out
across a thousand lifetimes
would you answer?
If I beckoned across the planes of thens and nows
would you acknowledge me?
If we are soulmates <u>then</u>,
where are you <u>now</u>?
Perhaps you cry to me
but I don't hear;
you beckon
but I don't see.
How many lifetimes
before we connect?
Perhaps we've met,
but one lifetime too soon.
I say to you <u>then</u>
from me <u>now</u>,
dare to dream,
and we will fly
Across a Thousand Lifetimes.

Night in Arizona

The moon is a charring ember
Dying into the eyes of dark;
Off in the crouching mountains
Coyotes bark.

The stars are heavy in heaven,
Too great for the sky to hold—
What if they fell and shattered
The earth with gold?

No lights are over the mesa,
The wind is hard and wild,
I stand at the darkened window
And cry like a child.

When All Your Dreams Have Left You

Watching summer clouds go floating by
thinking how the years have done the same
like a drifter thrown into the wind
the only thing that I own is my name

In a time when no one understood
what it's like to be a man without a dream
I threw my heart into your stormy eyes
and threw my gold into the fire to see it gleam

So don't you look at me and turn away
as if you can't abide the thoughts I bring to mind
'cause I'll be here for you to hold
when all your dreams have left you far behind

I used to have it all or so I thought
and everything I had I gave to you
but I didn't know when to let go
so you turned those restless eyes to someone new

I hear the two of you are doing well
as the one of me grows colder every day
but when his roaming hands hold someone else
just turn your heart around and look my way

So don't you look at me and turn away
as if you can't abide the thoughts I bring to mind
'cause I'll be here for you to hold
when all your dreams have left you far behind

Winter Ballet

Skaters leap and twirl
scars in patterns on the ice.
Their silver blades
flash in the sun
leaving blue spots before my eyes.
The smell of the vendor's popcorn
turns my head.
A red-cheeked girl
buys a cup of hot chocolate.
Steam escapes
from the Styrofoam cup
in little wisps
as she drinks.
On the ice a couple dances.
The other skaters stop and watch.
The dance is elegant;
the dancers move in perfect synchronicity.
An old man
wipes tears from his eyes.
The dancers
slide to a stop and bow.
Applause and cheers
greet the end
of the Winter Ballet.

Grate Dreams

Benny is happy
to see his bed unused.
With a yellow-toothed grin
he lies on the iron grate where the heat rises.
He no longer fears the people.
Experience tells him they're harmless.
Some regard him with pity,
most simply ignore him.
Asleep, he dreams of
So much food he cannot eat it all.
He sees his handsome image
reflected in the emerald eyes
of the lady across the table.
His dreams flee
before the insistent tap of the billy club
on his one good shoe.
As Benny shuffles away
from his warm iron bed
he reluctantly surrenders the dream,
not of a hopeful future,
but the recollection
of a long-faded past.

Still Life

The half-eaten taco
from the dumpster wasn't bad.
If he could find some cardboard
for the hole in his shoe,
he would be all set.
He drains the last swallow
from an abandoned Heaven Hill bottle.
With a smirk,
he smashes it against the sidewalk,
taking delight in the iridescent shards.
Only a few steps now
to his favorite heating grate.
With a smile,
he feels in his pocket
for the candy bar
he found beside the taco.
It's good to be alive.

Another Cliched Nature Poem

Acid rain pours
but still redbird sings.
Does he not know he's doomed?
And who is he
that he should be so happy
when I am sad?
Oaks and maples are disappearing
but the squirrel chatters gaily.
Does he not care that we are dying?
And why must he be so busy
when I have not the will to move?
Even the weeping willow seems cheerful.
Why then must I be grim?
Maybe the answer breathes through the trees.
The wind, as everything,
passes on.

The Picture in Time

Storms abate
the journey slows
hopefully ending
Traveler
state to state
night by night
hoping the road leads to you
Following the unseen path
guided by your unwavering light
Solitary Wanderer
Watching
Crossing your wake
to be blessed
anointed
Sharing for a while
or always
the unscarring brilliance
of mingled spirits to be fastened
Together
to chase the moon
across the star-sprinkled vale of forever

Malicious Whispers

Malicious whispers herald discontent
Sick of others' scorn
She contemplates the bridge
There is freedom in the falling
The water
Silences the whispers
Mutes her cry of anguish
And hides
The only tear she ever shed.

Neon Strangers

The drizzle turning to snow
brings thoughts of you.
On a night like this
we met.
You looked like a Christmas angel
in the glow of the street lamp.
Your wind-tossed hair was shining wet.
Your reddened cheeks
Shone under your ice-blue eyes.
Your warm smile
belied the cold weather.
Hot coffee cups thawed our fingers
as we talked in the café.
We traded secrets and dreams
'til the sun relieved the neon.
Finally we parted,
you to your world, and I to mine.
Each a memory to the other,
a face without a name.

October

Long walks on cool autumn days
the sun plays hide and seek through the clouds
tree limbs dance in the wind
shadows follow me everywhere

Plumes of dust arise with each step
sunlight turns the dust to gold
the scent of wood smoke fills the air
brown leaves rustle in time with my movements

Scarecrows and jack-o-lanterns adorn yards and porches
Yellow shocks of corn stand guard in the fields
I look around expectantly
but not a black cat do I see

Shadows grow longer as the day begins to fade
jack-o-lanterns' evil grins will soon be illuminated
my breath becomes visible and chill bumps cover my arms
gray smoke spiraling from a chimney tells me I am home

Rebirth

I cry
for the brother who
suffers death by assimilation.
His heritage
drowns in a bottle of alcohol.
Mother Earth's tears
fill lakes and oceans,
cleansing
even in their misery.
Somewhere,
through the ages,
a white feather floats.
Guided by the wind,
Down to the mother,
it rests
in a young child's hand.

Everything

My fingers touch your face
as your eyes gather twilight.
This, for me,
is everything.
The world dissolves
in pink and orange around us.
No longer time and space
we float
on layers of joy.
No sadness
as the journey slowly ends
for we will fly again.
Laughing,
through tears of gladness
we return
to a world
made brighter by our smiles.

Alchemy in Flames (The Marriage Poem)

I grinned
while I dug my grave.
Pretending not to remember what you said,
I leapt
into the fire of your anger.
I emerged
charred and blackened, but smiling,
amazed at how much I absorbed.
Funny.
I, so timid,
leapt fearlessly into the flames.
I had thought
I would wither in the face of them.
But,
when the black shell crumbles,
I shall find myself newly forged.

For Lynn

Her hair spills over her shoulder
like a red waterfall.
Breathing puffy little clouds,
she makes snow angels on the hillside.
Her laughter echoes across the clearing
as she shakes the snow from her back.
Smiling,
her blue eyes tearful from the cold,
she leaves for tea and the fireplace.

Thoughts of You

Thoughts of you rush in
like winter winds through
a broken window pane.
Cold
Empty
Hurting
The warmth of the sun
seems distant,
unreachable.
The warmth of your touch
is just as far,
and the loss
is much greater.
Cold
Empty
Hurting

My Friend

I'll put out my hand.
Take it, if you want.
I'll be your friend,
You be mine.
We can sit and talk.
We can just be still.
Friend we can dance!

Poet's Wine

Words flow from your pen,
but not your soul.
Phrases come,
as quick as a metronome's tick.
But not heartfelt.
They merely occupy the page.
Eyes full of pretension,
you proclaim yourself the Poet.
But your empty verses speak to no one.
Epic poems that sometimes rhyme,
profoundly unfounded.
You scribble poems on restaurant napkins,
hoping to seduce the simple waitress.
Scribbling fantasies
you drink your beer too quickly,
longing for the bittersweet taste
of the poet's wine.

Rain

Raindrops plunge from above
like cold tears from gray eyes
they pelt my face
and race down it like tiny rivers

My body shivers as the wind rises
needles of cold pierce my skin
water seeps through the hole in my shoe
I squint my toes to straighten my droopy sock

I begin to run as the rain falls harder
my bulletin jacket billows behind like a cape
my feet plop into pools of gathered teardrops
further soaking the sides of my legs

Thunder reverberates in my ears
lightning illuminates the blackened sky
ahead, my Chevy Mazda, a silver lining for dark clouds
I stop and reach for my keys………..My Keys!

Gemini

Trying to find myself
I see two images,
not mirrored, but
diametrically opposed.
Pulling against each other,
facing different destinies.
A turn leaves me in the same place,
staring at the same paths
through different eyes.
If each self could step backward
perhaps we would see eye to eye.
Or maybe we would only crash
and go down hard.
If only I could step forward
without impact.
Looking ahead, seeing behind,
afraid to move,
stillness.....

With Me

Come and sit with me on the river bank.
We'll look at the fish and turtles
and each other, and not talk for hours.
We'll starve away the sun, just you and

I

Come and run with me under the low hanging stars.
We'll dance and play on the wet summer grass.
We'll sing beneath the bright sickle moon,
of hopes and dreams and surely of

LOVE

Come and watch the years pass with me.
We'll grow old holding hands and
dancing in the twilight, and
all my dreams, awake or asleep, shall be of

YOU

Flying Too Close to the Sun

Like foolish Icarus,
I fear I'm flying too close
to the sun of your playful smile.
My wings of freedom melt
under the gaze of your deep coquettish eyes
Let me fall from the coveted heights of your regard,
to drown in the roiling sea of my obsession.
Let me fly at my own height,
and join me there if you will.
And one heartbeat at a time,
lift me up
to kiss the sun.

Emotional Hypothermia

The air outside is bitter cold,
reflecting my soul at the moment.
Just a touch
and it might shatter
into jagged shards.
One kind breath from you
would warm it back to life.
But looking into those ice blue eyes
the first crack forms.
With your first word
the mirror shatters,
ripping shrapnel through my guts.
So this is what I am,
A tiny piece of glass
Crushed beneath your heel.

Christine's Moon

Tonight
the moon glows like a promise whispered in the dark.
If you miss me too
close your eyes and pretend
that I am the man in the moon,
so that I might touch your windswept hair
and caress your cheek with soft lunar fingers.
Imagine the stars
are flaming arrows I shot at the night,
to pin our dreams to the black curtain sky.
And know that the moon is yours.
Until you came
there was no one to give it to,
at least no one I wanted to have it.
Now I give it to you
to bathe your nights in softness,
and paint your dreamscapes
with ambient light.

Annie's Lives, Part I:
Of Sunshine and Angels' Wings

Mommy's little Annie
Pulls the pink bow from her chestnut hair.
She's fourteen now
and far too old for such nonsense.
With her few possessions
and her teenage confidence
packed in a ragged gray duffel,
she slips through her window into the freezing rain . . .
She's walked so long now
her bones are made of ice.
A hundred steps
and a swallow of pride away from shelter,
she stops, blinded by headlights . . .
With the heat covering her like a grandmother's quilt,
and the kind man's voice
a whispering sedative,
Annie dreams
of sunshine and angels' wings.

Annie's Lives, Part II:
Mother

The old-looking young girl
with chestnut hair reaches for the needle.
Another tiny bee sting
and that faraway look returns
to annihilate the memory of another John
thumping down the stairs.
MOTHER,
seems such a holy word now,
one she longs for but dares not Profane
with her whiskey-stained voice.
The steps pop and crack
under some heavy man's weight.
Vaguely she wonders
if it's another nameless Phallus,
or her pimp come to get his share.
MOTHER,
do you miss me too?
The door is open.
An old man with firm gray eyes
approaches her bed . . .

Annie's Lives, Part III:
Hell

All Hallows Eve
when the dead come out to play.
The moon hangs like a severed head
and somewhere
an animal screams at the altar.
Annie fights to wake from this nightmare,
only to realize she isn't asleep.
Her soul bleeds
for thirteen and virginity,
when she was ignorant of Black Masses.
An icy pale hand on her cheek
brings her back to hell.
It's midnight
and Satan wants to dance.

Annie's Lives, Part IV:
Asylum

Flushed clean of crystal meth
she'd still die for a cigarette,
but the nice doctors tell her no.
The games are fun here at the asylum,
and she can dance when she feels like it.
She thinks of the older lady who sometimes visits,
and how the pink bow the woman gave her
stirs a vague remembrance.
Odd how the lady calls herself mother,
but maybe she's got problems too.
The doctors say if she's good
she can go home soon,
but she's not quite sure where home is;
maybe the lady can show her.
She winds the pink bow
through her slender fingers,
and for an instant recalls
fourteen and freezing rain.

Annie's Lives, Part V:
The Past Is Just That

In a tiny hospital in Vermont,
a pretty worker hums softly as
she pushes the food cart.
Three more rooms,
and she trades the medical whites
for faded jeans
and green Chuck Taylor sneakers.
It seems a lifetime ago that
she was a patient in a ward
much like this one.
It feels like years ago when
the lady who calls herself mother
saw her smile for the first time.
Life is good now.
The past is just that
and the future pregnant with hope.
She must hurry now or she'll be late for class.
Time to ponder her life later,
as she makes dinner for her mother.
One last moment to straighten
the pink bow in her chestnut hair,
and she bursts through the door
into the sunshine
and smiles at the familiar thought
of angels' wings.

Anastasia

If you could speak
from the painting
what would you say?
That the gold trim on your green dress
is scratching your delicate white shoulder?
That the scarlet posies
look better in the painting
than they ever could in real life?
That the poesy
tucked in your reddish brown hair
is too sweet for your wild tastes?
No words pass from your lips
but you speak to me.
Your expression speaks of royalty,
perhaps a prince's favorite daughter.
Your hair mirrors your personality.
Perfectly formed
but for the small rebellious curl.

An Evening Remembered

Hunan,
a pleasant haven from indecisive rain.
A place to talk of cool ghosts
over hot tea.
To delight in goosebumps
raised by stories of haunting ravens.
Our vines of conversation were green with promise,
and thoughts hung between us
like grapes
waiting to be plucked.
We spoke of conversation
and complained of complaining,
and laughed a great deal.
At last
the vines were empty (that's the nature of vines)
and we made our way back
to Mundania,
where the rain (I swear)
tasted like homemade wine.

Ageless Valentines

Memories of sweet chocolates by an open fireplace,
and drawing twin hearts on frosted windowpanes.
Outside, two snow angels held hands
in the soft winter snow, while inside
two lovers danced to the music only they could hear.
Their hair was as white as the world outside
but their hearts were as ageless as Cupid's archery.
And when the dances were danced,
and the Whitman's sampler lay empty by the fire,
the lovers kissed away the twilight and
held each other as the night embraced the falling snow.

You Bring the Sun

You bring the golden sun of May
into the darkest room,
And no spring flowers
ever seemed so fair as you.
Until you came,
I never heard the laughter
in the summer rain,
or listened to the poetry
whispered in the falling leaves.
In the heart's darkest winter,
You bring the sun.

When Words Lie Sleeping

When all the words lie sleeping on the page,
are any left to be spoken?
only these:
For a time,
our separate drummers coaxed a matching
rhythm
from our delicate drums.
And in that wordless moment,
the concert hall shone golden.

To Penny and Wes

When love transcends poetry
words are only inkblots
staining the page.
No need to write of crystal moons
when the light of merging souls
shatters the darkness
into a million flaming stars.
And who would dare to write
of two voices
locked in a passionate harmony
only lovers hear?
Yes, love can silence
even the most delicate muse,
until the only poetry left
is whispered
in the joining of two sighing hearts.

Poet's Moon

Tonight, the moon isn't a poet's moon.
It isn't a perfect silver disc hanging on fluffy
black curtains. Nor is it a pastel ball,
suspended at the top of its arc, waiting
for the down fall. It isn't half eaten,
nor a quicksilver scythe, poised to slice into
the black sky. It's merely an ordinary
partial moon, playing hide and seek in
the translucent gray clouds, floating ever
upward, breaking free from one
cloud-prison only to be captured briefly by another.
Nothing to write about at all.

Night Music

She moves like hard rock
on a classical guitar.
Her feet tattoo a rhythm into the cobblestones
While her arms conduct their own private symphony.
Her eyes pull down a pale blue harmony
and her hair trails behind,
a shimmering auburn glissando.
To applaud would break the spell,
so silently I watch
as the visual concert unfolds.
The music swells into a blinding crescendo,
then fades
as streetlights flood the stage.
Finally,
the last movement blends into the darkness,
leaving healed silence in its wake.

Just for Chris

I love to look into your eyes,
the color of evening blue, just before twilight.
I long to touch your soft hair,
shiny as new pennies spent on sweet lemon drops.
I live to hear your laughter
ringing in the air like breeze-kissed chimes.
I want to sing and dance
and play with you in the soft cotton snowfall.
Fly with me and I will hold your hand,
write you sonnets, and wrap your world in hugs and kisses.

Inside

Two men speak inside my head
to which one should I listen
Choices to make, I wait instead
for one voice to choose

One small cut and two souls bleed
which to bandage first
Anger and sadness both in need
one is hunger, the other thirst

You could play a lover's part
heal the wound inside of me
together we are one soul one heart
one mind one destiny

Inside I'm my own best friend
inside lies my enemy
the battleground is me again
war torn dichotomy

Can you help me find my way
to heart and soul and mind
I want to see the sun today
leave all the storms behind

You could play a lover's part
heal the wound inside of me
together we are one soul one heart
one mind one destiny

In Between

That space
between inhale and exhale
is eternity. That moment
when I am neither gaining nor losing,
just being,
is what I live for.
The moment after thunder,
when the oak is framed in lightning flash blue
and the world pauses in frozen color,
is why I breathe.
Events have significance
because of the spaces between.
Life too, has significance
in the stillness between laughter and tears,
when good and bad are lost in silence
and only breath remains.

If I Never See You Again

If I never see you again
Thank you for feeding me
with your last two dollars.
And thanks for
sharing the warm bluish light of
your gas stove when
you had no electricity.
If I never see you again
thank you for teaching me
John Prine songs on
your handmade Alvarez.
And thanks for
holding my hand when
I got drunk in Louisville.
If I never see you again
thank you for being my brother.

Good Morning

The world sucks at 7:00 a.m.
I run into the walls and can't complete a sentence
my mouth tastes like last night's hamburger
I try to replace my blood with caffeine.

My vocabulary consists of four-letter words
Some well-known, some invented on the spot
I start to stretch but get a headrush
I stagger and sway until the feeling passes.

I try to put on my clothes but they fight back
Oh well, maybe I'll leave my shirt on backwards
My heart stops as the alarm blasts
I always forget to turn the *********thing off!

Well, that alarm clock was getting old anyway
and there aren't too many pieces to clean up
of course the hole in the wall will need patching
Did I tell you that the world sucks at 7:00 a.m.?

East Panda Philosophy

Sitting in the East Panda
We discussed existentialism
between mouthfuls of lo mein and rice.
Outside, buildings melted into the heat
like a Dali painting
framed by the window.
We talked of art and music,
and you told me the secret
of drawing human feet.
Ideas were offered, then discarded,
as we were certain
only of our uncertainty.
Of one thing I was sure:
this small moment
was worth the risk
of fate or existentialism.

Of Kip and Kindness—A Lullaby for You

    I want to write a poem for you, Kip, with images so clear and full, they will keep your breath here.
    Like you coming down the street with your bag of responsibilities on your shoulder, giving a wave from the elbow, a wry tilt of your head, and a smile, and saying, "Hey, guys," a tad shy of knowing how glad we all are to see you.
    Like you rocking back and forth backstage three minutes before your cue, ready to dash onstage when it came.
    Like you noticing that eight-year-old Phoebe was sad or tired or bored, so you touch her shoulder and without a word she turns, and you both hug in a deep understanding of and taking comfort in each other.
    Like you sitting on Jeremy's deck, offering your famous toast "Troxy Clank of the Clan McClank!" and we all raise our beers and our smiles.
    Like you telling us about Ireland until it shines in your blue eyes and your curly black hair.
    Like you and music—Mary Black and a new guitar—and a kindness you have brought to this world that will never leave, for its impression has been left on all of us.

                      —by Naomi Buck

Order Form

To order additional copies, fill out this form and send it along with your check or money order to: Cheryl Perkins, 959 Apple Grove Road, Summer Shade, KY 42166.

Cost per copy $7.95 plus $2.00 P&H. If shipped to an address in Kentucky, include 6% state sales tax.

Ship _____ copies of *His Kentucky Smile And an Ireland Dream* to:

Name_____

Address:_____

Address:_____

Address:_____